AF481230

Clinical Notes

Name: ____

Year: ____

Roll No: ____

Department : ___________________________Unit: ______________

INDEX

Case No.	Case details	Page No.

Case Record Template

Patient Name :   Age :   Gender: IP No :

Occupation :   Address:

Chief Complaints:

1.

2.

3.

History of Present Illness:

History of Present Illness

Past History

☐ Hypertension (_____ yrs)
☐ Diabetes Mellitus (_____ yrs)
☐ Tuberculosis (_____ yrs)
☐ Bronchial Asthma / COPD (_____ yrs)
☐ ischemic heart disease (_____ yrs)
☐ Stroke / TIA (_____ yrs)
☐ Seizure Disorder (_____ yrs)
☐ Chronic kidney disease (_____ yrs)
☐ Others: __________ _____________________ ___________________

☐ Thyroid Disorders (_____ yrs)
☐ Hepatitis / Liver Disease (_____ yrs)
☐ Malignancy (Specify): __________ (_____ yrs)
☐ Previous Surgeries: _______ (Year: _______)
☐ Hospitalizations: __________ (Year: _______)
☐ Allergies (Drugs/Food): __________
☐ Blood Transfusions: _______ (Year: _____)

____

____

Personal History

☐ Marital Status: ☐ Single ☐ Married ☐ Widowed ☐ Divorced
Addictions:
☐ Smoking (_____ yrs) (Type / Quantity): ______________________________
☐ Alcohol (_____ yrs) (Type / Quantity): _________________________ CAGE : _______
☐ Others (Specify): ____ (_____ yrs)
☐ Dietary pattern: ☐ Vegetarian ☐ non-vegetarian
☐ Physical activity: ☐ Sedentary ☐ Moderate ☐ Active
☐ Others : __________ _____________________ ___________________________
____ (_____ yrs)

Menstrual & Obstetric History (if applicable)

☐ Age at menarche: __________ years
☐ Cycle length: __________ days
☐ Duration of bleeding: __________ days
☐ Regular cycles: ☐ Yes ☐ No
☐ Presence of clots: ☐ Yes ☐ No
☐ Obstetric history: G__ P__ L__ A__
☐ Last menstrual period (LMP): __________
☐ Menopause: ☐ Not attained ☐ Attained (age: _____ yrs)
Other : ____

☐ Dysmenorrhea: ☐ Mild ☐ Moderate ☐ Severe
☐ Intermenstrual bleeding: ☐ Yes ☐ No
☐ Vaginal discharge: ☐ Yes (Describe): __________ ☐ No

____

Family History

☐ Hypertension (Relation: ___________)

☐ Diabetes Mellitus (Relation: __________)

☐ Coronary Artery Disease (Relation: ______)

☐ Stroke (Relation: __________)

☐ Others: ____

☐ Epilepsy (Relation: __________)

☐ Tuberculosis (Relation: __________)

☐ Cancer (Specify / Relation): __________

☐ Genetic / Inherited Disorders: __________

Drug History

☐ Regular medication use:

☐ Antihypertensives (_____ yrs)

☐ Antidiabetics (_____ yrs)

☐ Steroids (_____ yrs)

☐ Antiepileptics (_____ yrs)

☐ Anticoagulants / Antiplatelets (_____ yrs)

☐ Drug allergies (Specify): ____

☐ Immunosuppressants (_____ yrs)

☐ Others: __________ (_____ yrs)

☐ Over-the-counter medications (_____ yrs)

☐ Herbal / Alternative medicines (_____ yrs)

☐ Recent change in medications (Specify):

____

Summary :

Differential Diagnosis:

1. _______________________________

2. _______________________________

3. _______________________________

General Examination

☐ Conscious ☐ Drowsy ☐ Unconscious

☐ Coherent ☐ Incoherent

☐ Pallor: ☐ Present ☐ Absent

☐ Icterus: ☐ Present ☐ Absent

☐ Cyanosis: ☐ Present ☐ Absent

☐ Other findings: ____

☐ Clubbing: ☐ Present (Grade: ___) ☐ Absent

☐ Pedal Edema: ☐ Present ☐ Absent

☐ Generalized Lymphadenopathy: ☐ Present ☐ Absent

Vitals

- Pulse: ___________ /min, ____ Regular/Irregular, ____ Rhythm, ____ Volume, ____ Character, ☐ All peripheral pulses felt, ☐ No radio-radial delay, ☐ No radio-femoral delay, Other findings: _____________________
- Blood Pressure: ___________ mmHg
- Respiratory Rate: __________ /min
- Temperature: __________ °C
- SpO_2 (on room air): __________ %

Systemic Examination:

1. **Inspection:**

2. **Palpation:**

3. **Percussion:**

2. **Auscultation:**

3. **Other System Examination:**

Provisional Diagnosis:

Plan of Management:

Investigations :

Treatment :

Discussion

Case Record Template

<table>
<tr><td>Patient Name :</td><td>Age :</td><td>Gender:</td><td>IP No :</td></tr>
<tr><td>Occupation :</td><td colspan="3">Address:</td></tr>
</table>

Chief Complaints:

1.

2.

3.

History of Present Illness:

History of Present Illness

Past History

☐ Hypertension (_____ yrs)
☐ Diabetes Mellitus (_____ yrs)
☐ Tuberculosis (_____ yrs)
☐ Bronchial Asthma / COPD (_____ yrs)
☐ ischemic heart disease (_____ yrs)
☐ Stroke / TIA (_____ yrs)
☐ Seizure Disorder (_____ yrs)
☐ Chronic kidney disease (_____ yrs)
☐ Others: ____

☐ Thyroid Disorders (_____ yrs)
☐ Hepatitis / Liver Disease (_____ yrs)
☐ Malignancy (Specify): __________ (_____ yrs)
☐ Previous Surgeries: _______ (Year: _______)
☐ Hospitalizations: _________ (Year: _______)
☐ Allergies (Drugs/Food): __________
☐ Blood Transfusions: _______ (Year: _____)

____

____

Personal History

☐ Marital Status: ☐ Single ☐ Married ☐ Widowed ☐ Divorced
Addictions:
☐ Smoking (_____ yrs) (Type / Quantity): ____
☐ Alcohol (_____ yrs) (Type / Quantity): ______________________________________ CAGE : _______
☐ Others (Specify): ____ (_____ yrs)
☐ Dietary pattern: ☐ Vegetarian ☐ non-vegetarian
☐ Physical activity: ☐ Sedentary ☐ Moderate ☐ Active
☐ Others : ____

____ (_____ yrs)

Menstrual & Obstetric History (if applicable)

☐ Age at menarche: __________ years
☐ Cycle length: __________ days
☐ Duration of bleeding: __________ days
☐ Regular cycles: ☐ Yes ☐ No
☐ Presence of clots: ☐ Yes ☐ No
☐ Obstetric history: G__ P__ L__ A__
☐ Last menstrual period (LMP): __________
☐ Menopause: ☐ Not attained ☐ Attained (age: _____ yrs)
Other : ____

☐ Dysmenorrhea: ☐ Mild ☐ Moderate ☐ Severe
☐ Intermenstrual bleeding: ☐ Yes ☐ No
☐ Vaginal discharge: ☐ Yes (Describe): __________ ☐ No

____

Family History

☐ Hypertension (Relation: ___________)   ☐ Epilepsy (Relation: ___________)

☐ Diabetes Mellitus (Relation: __________)   ☐ Tuberculosis (Relation: __________)

☐ Coronary Artery Disease (Relation: ______)   ☐ Cancer (Specify / Relation): __________

☐ Stroke (Relation: __________)   ☐ Genetic / Inherited Disorders: __________

☐ Others: ____

Drug History

☐ Regular medication use: ☐ Immunosuppressants (____ yrs)

☐ Antihypertensives (____ yrs)   ☐ Others: __________ (____ yrs)

☐ Antidiabetics (____ yrs)   ☐ Over-the-counter medications (____ yrs)

☐ Steroids (____ yrs)   ☐ Herbal / Alternative medicines (____ yrs)

☐ Antiepileptics (____ yrs)   ☐ Recent change in medications (Specify):

☐ Anticoagulants / Antiplatelets (____ yrs)   _______________________________

☐ Drug allergies (Specify): ____

Summary :

<table>
<tr><td>

Differential Diagnosis:

1. _______________________

2. _______________________

3. _______________________

</td></tr>
</table>

General Examination

☐ Conscious ☐ Drowsy ☐ Unconscious

☐ Coherent ☐ Incoherent

☐ Pallor: ☐ Present ☐ Absent

☐ Icterus: ☐ Present ☐ Absent

☐ Cyanosis: ☐ Present ☐ Absent

☐ Other findings: ____

☐ Clubbing: ☐ Present (Grade: ___) ☐ Absent

☐ Pedal Edema: ☐ Present ☐ Absent

☐ Generalized Lymphadenopathy: ☐ Present ☐ Absent

Vitals

- Pulse: ___________ /min, _____ Regular/Irregular, _____ Rhythm, _____ Volume, _____ Character, ☐ All peripheral pulses felt, ☐ No radio-radial delay, ☐ No radio-femoral delay, Other findings: _____________________
- Blood Pressure: ___________ mmHg
- Respiratory Rate: ___________ /min
- Temperature: ___________ °C
- SpO_2 (on room air): ___________ %

Systemic Examination:

1. **Inspection:**

2. **Palpation:**

3. **Percussion:**

4. **Auscultation:**

5. **Other System Examination:**

Provisional Diagnosis:

Plan of Management:

Investigations :

Treatment :

Discussion

Case Record Template

<table>
<tr><td>Patient Name :</td><td>Age :</td><td>Gender:</td><td>IP No :</td></tr>
<tr><td>Occupation :</td><td colspan="3">Address:</td></tr>
</table>

Chief Complaints:

1.

2.

3.

History of Present Illness:

History of Present Illness

Past History

☐ Hypertension (_____ yrs)
☐ Diabetes Mellitus (_____ yrs)
☐ Tuberculosis (_____ yrs)
☐ Bronchial Asthma / COPD (_____ yrs)
☐ ischemic heart disease (_____ yrs)
☐ Stroke / TIA (_____ yrs)
☐ Seizure Disorder (_____ yrs)
☐ Chronic kidney disease (_____ yrs)
☐ Others: ___________ _______________________ ___________________________________

☐ Thyroid Disorders (_____ yrs)
☐ Hepatitis / Liver Disease (_____ yrs)
☐ Malignancy (Specify): __________ (_____ yrs)
☐ Previous Surgeries: _______ (Year: _______)
☐ Hospitalizations: __________ (Year: _______)
☐ Allergies (Drugs/Food): ___________
☐ Blood Transfusions: _______ (Year: _____)

_________ __________________________ __ ______________________ _______

_________ ___________ ________________ ___

Personal History

☐ Marital Status: ☐ Single ☐ Married ☐ Widowed ☐ Divorced
Addictions:
☐ Smoking (_____ yrs) (Type / Quantity): ____
☐ Alcohol (_____ yrs) (Type / Quantity): _________________________________ CAGE : _______
☐ Others (Specify): ____ (_____ yrs)
☐ Dietary pattern: ☐ Vegetarian ☐ non-vegetarian
☐ Physical activity: ☐ Sedentary ☐ Moderate ☐ Active
☐ Others : ___________ ________________________ ___________________________________
____ (_____ yrs)

Menstrual & Obstetric History (if applicable)

☐ Age at menarche: ___________ years
☐ Cycle length: ___________ days
☐ Duration of bleeding: ___________ days
☐ Regular cycles: ☐ Yes ☐ No
☐ Presence of clots: ☐ Yes ☐ No
☐ Obstetric history: G__ P__ L__ A__
☐ Last menstrual period (LMP): ___________
☐ Menopause: ☐ Not attained ☐ Attained (age: _____ yrs)
Other : ___________________________________

☐ Dysmenorrhea: ☐ Mild ☐ Moderate ☐ Severe
☐ Intermenstrual bleeding: ☐ Yes ☐ No
☐ Vaginal discharge: ☐ Yes (Describe): ___________ ☐ No

Family History

☐ Hypertension (Relation: ____________) ☐ Epilepsy (Relation: ____________)

☐ Diabetes Mellitus (Relation: __________) ☐ Tuberculosis (Relation: __________)

☐ Coronary Artery Disease (Relation: ______) ☐ Cancer (Specify / Relation): __________

☐ Stroke (Relation: __________) ☐ Genetic / Inherited Disorders: __________

☐ Others: ____

Drug History

☐ Regular medication use: ☐ Immunosuppressants (_____ yrs)

☐ Antihypertensives (_____ yrs) ☐ Others: __________ (_____ yrs)

☐ Antidiabetics (_____ yrs) ☐ Over-the-counter medications (_____ yrs)

☐ Steroids (_____ yrs) ☐ Herbal / Alternative medicines (_____ yrs)

☐ Antiepileptics (_____ yrs) ☐ Recent change in medications (Specify):

☐ Anticoagulants / Antiplatelets (_____ yrs) ____

☐ Drug allergies (Specify): ____

Summary :

Differential Diagnosis:

1. ________________________________

2. ________________________________

3. ________________________________

General Examination

☐ Conscious ☐ Drowsy ☐ Unconscious

☐ Coherent ☐ Incoherent

☐ Pallor: ☐ Present ☐ Absent

☐ Icterus: ☐ Present ☐ Absent

☐ Cyanosis: ☐ Present ☐ Absent

☐ Other findings: ____

☐ Clubbing: ☐ Present (Grade: ___) ☐ Absent

☐ Pedal Edema: ☐ Present ☐ Absent

☐ Generalized Lymphadenopathy: ☐ Present ☐ Absent

Vitals

- Pulse: __________ /min, ____ Regular/Irregular, ____ Rhythm, ____ Volume, ____ Character, ☐ All peripheral pulses felt, ☐ No radio-radial delay, ☐ No radio-femoral delay, Other findings: ___________________
- Blood Pressure: __________ mmHg
- Respiratory Rate: __________ /min
- Temperature: __________ °C
- SpO_2 (on room air): __________ %

Systemic Examination:

1. **Inspection:**

2. **Palpation:**

3. **Percussion:**

6. **Auscultation:**

7. **Other System Examination:**

Provisional Diagnosis:

Plan of Management:

Investigations :

Treatment :

Discussion

Case Record Template

Patient Name :   Age :   Gender: IP No :

Occupation :   Address:

Chief Complaints:

1.

2.

3.

History of Present Illness:

History of Present Illness

Past History

☐ Hypertension (_____ yrs)
☐ Diabetes Mellitus (_____ yrs)
☐ Tuberculosis (_____ yrs)
☐ Bronchial Asthma / COPD (_____ yrs)
☐ ischemic heart disease (_____ yrs)
☐ Stroke / TIA (_____ yrs)
☐ Seizure Disorder (_____ yrs)
☐ Chronic kidney disease (_____ yrs)
☐ Others: ____________ ____________ ____________________

☐ Thyroid Disorders (_____ yrs)
☐ Hepatitis / Liver Disease (_____ yrs)
☐ Malignancy (Specify): _________ (_____ yrs)
☐ Previous Surgeries: _______ (Year: ______)
☐ Hospitalizations: _________ (Year: ______)
☐ Allergies (Drugs/Food): __________
☐ Blood Transfusions: ______ (Year: _____)

____________ ________________________________ ________________ ________
_________ _________ ________________________ ________________________ ___

Personal History

☐ Marital Status: ☐ Single ☐ Married ☐ Widowed ☐ Divorced
Addictions:
☐ Smoking (_____ yrs) (Type / Quantity): ____
☐ Alcohol (_____ yrs) (Type / Quantity): __________________________________ CAGE : _______
☐ Others (Specify): ____ (_____ yrs)
☐ Dietary pattern: ☐ Vegetarian ☐ non-vegetarian
☐ Physical activity: ☐ Sedentary ☐ Moderate ☐ Active
☐ Others : __________ _____________________ ____________________________
____ (_____ yrs)

Menstrual & Obstetric History (if applicable)

☐ Age at menarche: ___________ years
☐ Cycle length: ___________ days
☐ Duration of bleeding: ___________ days
☐ Regular cycles: ☐ Yes ☐ No
☐ Presence of clots: ☐ Yes ☐ No
☐ Obstetric history: G__ P__ L__ A__
☐ Last menstrual period (LMP): ___________
☐ Menopause: ☐ Not attained ☐ Attained (age: _____ yrs)
Other : ____

☐ Dysmenorrhea: ☐ Mild ☐ Moderate ☐ Severe
☐ Intermenstrual bleeding: ☐ Yes ☐ No
☐ Vaginal discharge: ☐ Yes (Describe): ___________ ☐ No

____

Family History

☐ Hypertension (Relation: ___________)

☐ Diabetes Mellitus (Relation: ___________)

☐ Coronary Artery Disease (Relation: _______)

☐ Stroke (Relation: ___________)

☐ Others: ____

☐ Epilepsy (Relation: ___________)

☐ Tuberculosis (Relation: ___________)

☐ Cancer (Specify / Relation): ___________

☐ Genetic / Inherited Disorders: ___________

Drug History

☐ Regular medication use:

☐ Antihypertensives (____ yrs)

☐ Antidiabetics (____ yrs)

☐ Steroids (____ yrs)

☐ Antiepileptics (____ yrs)

☐ Anticoagulants / Antiplatelets (____ yrs)

☐ Drug allergies (Specify): ____

☐ Immunosuppressants (____ yrs)

☐ Others: ___________ (____ yrs)

☐ Over-the-counter medications (____ yrs)

☐ Herbal / Alternative medicines (____ yrs)

☐ Recent change in medications (Specify):

____

Summary :

Differential Diagnosis:

1. _______________________________

2. _______________________________

3. _______________________________

General Examination

☐ Conscious ☐ Drowsy ☐ Unconscious

☐ Coherent ☐ Incoherent

☐ Pallor: ☐ Present ☐ Absent

☐ Icterus: ☐ Present ☐ Absent

☐ Cyanosis: ☐ Present ☐ Absent

☐ Other findings: ____

☐ Clubbing: ☐ Present (Grade: ____) ☐ Absent

☐ Pedal Edema: ☐ Present ☐ Absent

☐ Generalized Lymphadenopathy: ☐ Present ☐ Absent

Vitals

- Pulse: ___________ /min, _____ Regular/Irregular, _____ Rhythm, _____ Volume, _____ Character, ☐ All peripheral pulses felt, ☐ No radio-radial delay, ☐ No radio-femoral delay, Other findings: ______________________
- Blood Pressure: __________ mmHg
- Respiratory Rate: __________ /min
- Temperature: _________ °C
- SpO_2 (on room air): __________ %

Systemic Examination:

1. **Inspection:**

2. **Palpation:**

3. **Percussion:**

8. **Auscultation:**

9. **Other System Examination:**

Provisional Diagnosis:

Plan of Management:

Investigations :

Treatment :

Discussion

Case Record Template

Patient Name :	**Age :**	**Gender:**	**IP No :**
Occupation :		**Address:**	

Chief Complaints:

1.

2.

3.

History of Present Illness:

History of Present Illness

Past History

☐ Hypertension (_____ yrs)
☐ Diabetes Mellitus (_____ yrs)
☐ Tuberculosis (_____ yrs)
☐ Bronchial Asthma / COPD (_____ yrs)
☐ ischemic heart disease (_____ yrs)
☐ Stroke / TIA (_____ yrs)
☐ Seizure Disorder (_____ yrs)
☐ Chronic kidney disease (_____ yrs)
☐ Others: _______________ _______________

☐ Thyroid Disorders (_____ yrs)
☐ Hepatitis / Liver Disease (_____ yrs)
☐ Malignancy (Specify): __________ (_____ yrs)
☐ Previous Surgeries: _______ (Year: _______)
☐ Hospitalizations: _________ (Year: _______)
☐ Allergies (Drugs/Food): __________
☐ Blood Transfusions: _______ (Year: _____)

_______________ _______________ _______________ _______________
_______________ _______________ _______________ _______________

Personal History

☐ Marital Status: ☐ Single ☐ Married ☐ Widowed ☐ Divorced
Addictions:
☐ Smoking (_____ yrs) (Type / Quantity): _______________________________
☐ Alcohol (_____ yrs) (Type / Quantity): _______________________ CAGE : _______
☐ Others (Specify): ____ (_____ yrs)
☐ Dietary pattern: ☐ Vegetarian ☐ non-vegetarian
☐ Physical activity: ☐ Sedentary ☐ Moderate ☐ Active
☐ Others : __________ _______________ _______________
____ (_____ yrs)

Menstrual & Obstetric History (if applicable)

☐ Age at menarche: __________ years
☐ Cycle length: __________ days
☐ Duration of bleeding: __________ days
☐ Regular cycles: ☐ Yes ☐ No
☐ Presence of clots: ☐ Yes ☐ No
☐ Obstetric history: G__ P__ L__ A__
☐ Last menstrual period (LMP): __________
☐ Menopause: ☐ Not attained ☐ Attained (age: _____ yrs)
Other : ____

☐ Dysmenorrhea: ☐ Mild ☐ Moderate ☐ Severe
☐ Intermenstrual bleeding: ☐ Yes ☐ No
☐ Vaginal discharge: ☐ Yes (Describe): __________ ☐ No

____

Family History

☐ Hypertension (Relation: ___________) ☐ Epilepsy (Relation: __________)

☐ Diabetes Mellitus (Relation: __________) ☐ Tuberculosis (Relation: __________)

☐ Coronary Artery Disease (Relation: ______) ☐ Cancer (Specify / Relation): __________

☐ Stroke (Relation: ___________) ☐ Genetic / Inherited Disorders: __________

☐ Others: ____

Drug History

☐ Regular medication use: ☐ Immunosuppressants (____ yrs)

☐ Antihypertensives (____ yrs) ☐ Others: __________ (____ yrs)

☐ Antidiabetics (____ yrs) ☐ Over-the-counter medications (____ yrs)

☐ Steroids (____ yrs) ☐ Herbal / Alternative medicines (____ yrs)

☐ Antiepileptics (____ yrs) ☐ Recent change in medications (Specify):

☐ Anticoagulants / Antiplatelets (____ yrs) ________________________________

☐ Drug allergies (Specify): ____

Summary :

Differential Diagnosis:

1. _______________________________

2. _______________________________

3. _______________________________

General Examination

☐ Conscious ☐ Drowsy ☐ Unconscious

☐ Coherent ☐ Incoherent

☐ Pallor: ☐ Present ☐ Absent

☐ Icterus: ☐ Present ☐ Absent

☐ Cyanosis: ☐ Present ☐ Absent

☐ Other findings: ____

☐ Clubbing: ☐ Present (Grade: ___) ☐ Absent

☐ Pedal Edema: ☐ Present ☐ Absent

☐ Generalized Lymphadenopathy: ☐ Present ☐ Absent

Vitals

- Pulse: ___________ /min, _____ Regular/Irregular, _____ Rhythm, _____ Volume, _____ Character, ☐ All peripheral pulses felt, ☐ No radio-radial delay, ☐ No radio-femoral delay, Other findings: ____________________
- Blood Pressure: ___________ mmHg
- Respiratory Rate: ___________ /min
- Temperature: ___________ °C
- SpO_2 (on room air): ___________ %

Systemic Examination:

1. **Inspection:**

2. **Palpation:**

3. **Percussion:**

10. **Auscultation:**

11. **Other System Examination:**

Provisional Diagnosis:

Plan of Management:

Investigations :

Treatment :

Discussion

Case Record Template

Patient Name :   Age :   Gender: IP No :

Occupation :   Address:

Chief Complaints:

1.

2.

3.

History of Present Illness:

History of Present Illness

Past History

☐ Hypertension (____ yrs)
☐ Diabetes Mellitus (____ yrs)
☐ Tuberculosis (____ yrs)
☐ Bronchial Asthma / COPD (____ yrs)
☐ ischemic heart disease (____ yrs)
☐ Stroke / TIA (____ yrs)
☐ Seizure Disorder (____ yrs)
☐ Chronic kidney disease (____ yrs)
☐ Others: ___________ _______________ ________________
___________ _______________ ___ ___________ ______
_________ _____ ______________ ____________ ___

☐ Thyroid Disorders (____ yrs)
☐ Hepatitis / Liver Disease (____ yrs)
☐ Malignancy (Specify): _________ (____ yrs)
☐ Previous Surgeries: _______ (Year: _______)
☐ Hospitalizations: _________ (Year: _______)
☐ Allergies (Drugs/Food): __________
☐ Blood Transfusions: _______ (Year: _____)

Personal History

☐ Marital Status: ☐ Single ☐ Married ☐ Widowed ☐ Divorced
Addictions:
☐ Smoking (____ yrs) (Type / Quantity): ___________________________
☐ Alcohol (____ yrs) (Type / Quantity): _______________________ CAGE : _______
☐ Others (Specify): ___________________________________ (____ yrs)
☐ Dietary pattern: ☐ Vegetarian ☐ non-vegetarian
☐ Physical activity: ☐ Sedentary ☐ Moderate ☐ Active
☐ Others : __________ _______________ ___________________
_______________________________________ (____ yrs)

Menstrual & Obstetric History (if applicable)

☐ Age at menarche: __________ years
☐ Cycle length: __________ days
☐ Duration of bleeding: __________ days
☐ Regular cycles: ☐ Yes ☐ No
☐ Presence of clots: ☐ Yes ☐ No
☐ Obstetric history: G__ P__ L__ A__
☐ Last menstrual period (LMP): __________
☐ Menopause: ☐ Not attained ☐ Attained (age: ____ yrs)
Other : ___________________________________
____

☐ Dysmenorrhea: ☐ Mild ☐ Moderate ☐ Severe
☐ Intermenstrual bleeding. ☐ Yes ☐ No
☐ Vaginal discharge: ☐ Yes (Describe): __________ ☐ No

Family History

☐ Hypertension (Relation: ___________)
☐ Diabetes Mellitus (Relation: __________)
☐ Coronary Artery Disease (Relation: ______)
☐ Stroke (Relation: __________)
☐ Others: ____

☐ Epilepsy (Relation: __________)
☐ Tuberculosis (Relation: __________)
☐ Cancer (Specify / Relation): __________
☐ Genetic / Inherited Disorders: __________

Drug History

☐ Regular medication use:
☐ Antihypertensives (_____ yrs)
☐ Antidiabetics (_____ yrs)
☐ Steroids (_____ yrs)
☐ Antiepileptics (_____ yrs)
☐ Anticoagulants / Antiplatelets (_____ yrs)
☐ Drug allergies (Specify): ____

☐ Immunosuppressants (_____ yrs)
☐ Others: __________ (_____ yrs)
☐ Over-the-counter medications (_____ yrs)
☐ Herbal / Alternative medicines (_____ yrs)
☐ Recent change in medications (Specify):
____

Summary :

<table><tr><td>

Differential Diagnosis:

1. _____________________

2. _____________________

3. _____________________

</td></tr></table>

General Examination

☐ Conscious ☐ Drowsy ☐ Unconscious

☐ Coherent ☐ Incoherent

☐ Pallor: ☐ Present ☐ Absent

☐ Icterus: ☐ Present ☐ Absent

☐ Cyanosis: ☐ Present ☐ Absent

☐ Other findings: ____

☐ Clubbing: ☐ Present (Grade: ___) ☐ Absent

☐ Pedal Edema: ☐ Present ☐ Absent

☐ Generalized Lymphadenopathy: ☐ Present ☐ Absent

Vitals

- Pulse: __________ /min, ____ Regular/Irregular, ____ Rhythm, ____ Volume, ____ Character, ☐ All peripheral pulses felt, ☐ No radio-radial delay, ☐ No radio-femoral delay, Other findings: ___________________
- Blood Pressure: __________ mmHg
- Respiratory Rate: __________ /min
- Temperature: __________ °C
- SpO_2 (on room air): __________ %

Systemic Examination:

1. **Inspection:**

2. **Palpation:**

3. **Percussion:**

12. **Auscultation:**

13. **Other System Examination:**

Provisional Diagnosis:

Plan of Management:

Investigations :

Treatment :

Discussion

Case Record Template

Patient Name :   Age : Gender: IP No :

Occupation :   Address:

Chief Complaints:

1.

2.

3.

History of Present Illness:

History of Present Illness

Past History

□ Hypertension (_____ yrs) □ Thyroid Disorders (_____ yrs)
□ Diabetes Mellitus (_____ yrs) □ Hepatitis / Liver Disease (_____ yrs)
□ Tuberculosis (_____ yrs) □ Malignancy (Specify): __________ (_____ yrs)
□ Bronchial Asthma / COPD (_____ yrs) □ Previous Surgeries: _______ (Year: _______)
□ ischemic heart disease (_____ yrs) □ Hospitalizations: __________ (Year: _______)
□ Stroke / TIA (_____ yrs) □ Allergies (Drugs/Food): ___________
□ Seizure Disorder (_____ yrs) □ Blood Transfusions: _______ (Year: ______)
□ Chronic kidney disease (_____ yrs)
□ Others: ___________ ______________________ _______________________

________________ ____________________________ __________ _________ __________

________________ ____________ ___________________ ___

Personal History

□ Marital Status: □ Single □ Married □ Widowed □ Divorced
Addictions:
□ Smoking (_____ yrs) (Type / Quantity): ______________________________________
□ Alcohol (_____ yrs) (Type / Quantity): ______________________________ CAGE : _______
□ Others (Specify): ______________________________________ (_____ yrs)
□ Dietary pattern: □ Vegetarian □ non-vegetarian
□ Physical activity: □ Sedentary □ Moderate □ Active
□ Others : ___________ ____________________ ______________________

____ (_____ yrs)

Menstrual & Obstetric History (if applicable)

□ Age at menarche: ___________ years □ Dysmenorrhea: □ Mild □ Moderate □ Severe
□ Cycle length: ___________ days □ Intermenstrual bleeding: □ Yes □ No
□ Duration of bleeding: ___________ days □ Vaginal discharge: □ Yes (Describe):
□ Regular cycles: □ Yes □ No ___________ □ No
□ Presence of clots: □ Yes □ No
□ Obstetric history: G__ P__ L__ A__
□ Last menstrual period (LMP): ___________
□ Menopause: □ Not attained □ Attained (age: _____ yrs)
Other : ____

____

Family History

☐ Hypertension (Relation: ___________)

☐ Diabetes Mellitus (Relation: __________)

☐ Coronary Artery Disease (Relation: ______)

☐ Stroke (Relation: __________)

☐ Epilepsy (Relation: __________)

☐ Tuberculosis (Relation: __________)

☐ Cancer (Specify / Relation): __________

☐ Genetic / Inherited Disorders: __________

☐ Others: ____

Drug History

☐ Regular medication use:

☐ Antihypertensives (_____ yrs)

☐ Antidiabetics (_____ yrs)

☐ Steroids (_____ yrs)

☐ Antiepileptics (_____ yrs)

☐ Anticoagulants / Antiplatelets (_____ yrs)

☐ Drug allergies (Specify): ____

☐ Immunosuppressants (_____ yrs)

☐ Others: __________ (_____ yrs)

☐ Over-the-counter medications (_____ yrs)

☐ Herbal / Alternative medicines (_____ yrs)

☐ Recent change in medications (Specify):

____

Summary :

Differential Diagnosis:

1. ___________________________

2. ___________________________

3. ___________________________

General Examination

☐ Conscious ☐ Drowsy ☐ Unconscious

☐ Coherent ☐ Incoherent

☐ Pallor: ☐ Present ☐ Absent

☐ Icterus: ☐ Present ☐ Absent

☐ Cyanosis: ☐ Present ☐ Absent

☐ Other findings: ____

☐ Clubbing: ☐ Present (Grade: ___) ☐ Absent

☐ Pedal Edema: ☐ Present ☐ Absent

☐ Generalized Lymphadenopathy: ☐ Present ☐ Absent

Vitals

- Pulse: ___________ /min, ____ Regular/Irregular, ____ Rhythm, ____ Volume, ____ Character, ☐ All peripheral pulses felt, ☐ No radio-radial delay, ☐ No radio-femoral delay, Other findings: ____________________
- Blood Pressure: ___________ mmHg
- Respiratory Rate: ___________ /min
- Temperature: ___________ °C
- SpO_2 (on room air): ___________ %

Systemic Examination:

1. **Inspection:**

2. **Palpation:**

3. **Percussion:**

14. **Auscultation:**

15. **Other System Examination:**

Provisional Diagnosis:

Plan of Management:

Investigations :

Treatment :

Discussion

Case Record Template

Patient Name :   **Age :**   **Gender:**   **IP No :**

Occupation :   **Address:**

Chief Complaints:

1.

2.

3.

History of Present Illness:

History of Present Illness

Past History

☐ Hypertension (_____ yrs)
☐ Diabetes Mellitus (_____ yrs)
☐ Tuberculosis (_____ yrs)
☐ Bronchial Asthma / COPD (_____ yrs)
☐ ischemic heart disease (_____ yrs)
☐ Stroke / TIA (_____ yrs)
☐ Seizure Disorder (_____ yrs)
☐ Chronic kidney disease (_____ yrs)
☐ Others: __________ __________________ ___________________________________

☐ Thyroid Disorders (_____ yrs)
☐ Hepatitis / Liver Disease (_____ yrs)
☐ Malignancy (Specify): _________ (_____ yrs)
☐ Previous Surgeries: _______ (Year: _______)
☐ Hospitalizations: _________ (Year: _______)
☐ Allergies (Drugs/Food): __________
☐ Blood Transfusions: _______ (Year: _____)

_______________ _______________________ __ _____________ _________ ______

_________ ___________________ ___________________________ _________ ___

Personal History

☐ Marital Status: ☐ Single ☐ Married ☐ Widowed ☐ Divorced
Addictions:
☐ Smoking (_____ yrs) (Type / Quantity): ______________________________________
☐ Alcohol (_____ yrs) (Type / Quantity): ________________________ CAGE :_______
☐ Others (Specify): ____ (_____ yrs)
☐ Dietary pattern: ☐ Vegetarian ☐ non-vegetarian
☐ Physical activity: ☐ Sedentary ☐ Moderate ☐ Active
☐ Others : __________ _______________________ _______________________
____ (_____ yrs)

Menstrual & Obstetric History (if applicable)

☐ Age at menarche: __________ years
☐ Cycle length: __________ days
☐ Duration of bleeding: __________ days
☐ Regular cycles: ☐ Yes ☐ No
☐ Presence of clots: ☐ Yes ☐ No
☐ Obstetric history: G__ P__ L__ A__
☐ Last menstrual period (LMP): __________
☐ Menopause: ☐ Not attained ☐ Attained (age: _____ yrs)
Other : ____

☐ Dysmenorrhea: ☐ Mild ☐ Moderate ☐ Severe
☐ Intermenstrual bleeding: ☐ Yes ☐ No
☐ Vaginal discharge: ☐ Yes (Describe): __________ ☐ No

____

Family History

☐ Hypertension (Relation: ___________)

☐ Diabetes Mellitus (Relation: ___________)

☐ Coronary Artery Disease (Relation: _______)

☐ Stroke (Relation: ___________)

☐ Others: ____

☐ Epilepsy (Relation: ___________)

☐ Tuberculosis (Relation: ___________)

☐ Cancer (Specify / Relation): ___________

☐ Genetic / Inherited Disorders: ___________

Drug History

☐ Regular medication use:

☐ Antihypertensives (_____ yrs)

☐ Antidiabetics (_____ yrs)

☐ Steroids (_____ yrs)

☐ Antiepileptics (_____ yrs)

☐ Anticoagulants / Antiplatelets (_____ yrs)

☐ Drug allergies (Specify): ____

☐ Immunosuppressants (_____ yrs)

☐ Others: ___________ (_____ yrs)

☐ Over-the-counter medications (_____ yrs)

☐ Herbal / Alternative medicines (_____ yrs)

☐ Recent change in medications (Specify):

____

Summary :

Differential Diagnosis:

1. _________________________________

2. _________________________________

3. _________________________________

General Examination

☐ Conscious ☐ Drowsy ☐ Unconscious

☐ Coherent ☐ Incoherent

☐ Pallor: ☐ Present ☐ Absent

☐ Icterus: ☐ Present ☐ Absent

☐ Cyanosis: ☐ Present ☐ Absent

☐ Other findings: ____

☐ Clubbing: ☐ Present (Grade: ___) ☐ Absent

☐ Pedal Edema: ☐ Present ☐ Absent

☐ Generalized Lymphadenopathy: ☐ Present ☐ Absent

Vitals

- Pulse: __________ /min, _____ Regular/Irregular, _____ Rhythm, _____ Volume, _____ Character, ☐ All peripheral pulses felt, ☐ No radio-radial delay, ☐ No radio-femoral delay, Other findings: ____________________
- Blood Pressure: __________ mmHg
- Respiratory Rate: __________ /min
- Temperature: __________ °C
- SpO_2 (on room air): __________ %

Systemic Examination:

1. **Inspection:**

2. **Palpation:**

3. **Percussion:**

16. **Auscultation:**

17. **Other System Examination:**

Provisional Diagnosis:

Plan of Management:

Investigations :

Treatment :

Discussion

<h1 align="center">Case Record Template</h1>

<table>
<tr><td>Patient Name :</td><td>Age :</td><td>Gender:</td><td>IP No :</td></tr>
<tr><td>Occupation :</td><td colspan="3">Address:</td></tr>
</table>

Chief Complaints:

1.

2.

3.

History of Present Illness:

History of Present Illness

Past History

☐ Hypertension (_____ yrs)   ☐ Thyroid Disorders (_____ yrs)

☐ Diabetes Mellitus (_____ yrs)   ☐ Hepatitis / Liver Disease (_____ yrs)

☐ Tuberculosis (_____ yrs)   ☐ Malignancy (Specify): __________ (_____ yrs)

☐ Bronchial Asthma / COPD (_____ yrs)   ☐ Previous Surgeries: ________ (Year: _______)

☐ ischemic heart disease (_____ yrs)   ☐ Hospitalizations: __________ (Year: _______)

☐ Stroke / TIA (_____ yrs)   ☐ Allergies (Drugs/Food): ___________

☐ Seizure Disorder (_____ yrs)   ☐ Blood Transfusions: _______ (Year: ______)

☐ Chronic kidney disease (_____ yrs)

☐ Others: ___________ ______________________ ________________________________

_____________ _________________________ _______________________ ___________

____________ ____________ __________________ ________________________ _____

Personal History

☐ Marital Status: ☐ Single ☐ Married ☐ Widowed ☐ Divorced
Addictions:
☐ Smoking (_____ yrs) (Type / Quantity): ____

☐ Alcohol (_____ yrs) (Type / Quantity): ___________________________________ CAGE : _______

☐ Others (Specify): ____ (_____ yrs)

☐ Dietary pattern: ☐ Vegetarian ☐ non-vegetarian

☐ Physical activity: ☐ Sedentary ☐ Moderate ☐ Active

☐ Others : __________ ______________________ ____________________________

____ (_____ yrs)

Menstrual & Obstetric History (if applicable)

☐ Age at menarche: ___________ years   ☐ Dysmenorrhea: ☐ Mild ☐ Moderate ☐ Severe

☐ Cycle length: ___________ days   ☐ Intermenstrual bleeding: ☐ Yes ☐ No

☐ Duration of bleeding: ___________ days   ☐ Vaginal discharge: ☐ Yes (Describe): ___________ ☐ No

☐ Regular cycles: ☐ Yes ☐ No

☐ Presence of clots: ☐ Yes ☐ No

☐ Obstetric history: G__ P__ L__ A__

☐ Last menstrual period (LMP): ___________

☐ Menopause: ☐ Not attained ☐ Attained (age: _____ yrs)

Other : ____

____

Family History

☐ Hypertension (Relation: ___________)

☐ Diabetes Mellitus (Relation: __________)

☐ Coronary Artery Disease (Relation: ______)

☐ Stroke (Relation: ___________)

☐ Others: ____

☐ Epilepsy (Relation: __________)

☐ Tuberculosis (Relation: __________)

☐ Cancer (Specify / Relation): __________

☐ Genetic / Inherited Disorders: __________

Drug History

☐ Regular medication use:

☐ Antihypertensives (_____ yrs)

☐ Antidiabetics (_____ yrs)

☐ Steroids (_____ yrs)

☐ Antiepileptics (_____ yrs)

☐ Anticoagulants / Antiplatelets (_____ yrs)

☐ Drug allergies (Specify): ____

☐ Immunosuppressants (_____ yrs)

☐ Others: __________ (_____ yrs)

☐ Over-the-counter medications (_____ yrs)

☐ Herbal / Alternative medicines (_____ yrs)

☐ Recent change in medications (Specify):

____

Summary :

Differential Diagnosis:

1. _________________________________

2. _________________________________

3. _________________________________

General Examination

☐ Conscious ☐ Drowsy ☐ Unconscious

☐ Coherent ☐ Incoherent

☐ Pallor: ☐ Present ☐ Absent

☐ Icterus: ☐ Present ☐ Absent

☐ Cyanosis: ☐ Present ☐ Absent

☐ Other findings: ____

☐ Clubbing: ☐ Present (Grade: ___) ☐ Absent

☐ Pedal Edema: ☐ Present ☐ Absent

☐ Generalized Lymphadenopathy: ☐ Present ☐ Absent

Vitals

- Pulse: ___________ /min, _____ Regular/Irregular, _____ Rhythm, _____ Volume, _____ Character, ☐ All peripheral pulses felt, ☐ No radio-radial delay, ☐ No radio-femoral delay, Other findings: _______________________
- Blood Pressure: ___________ mmHg
- Respiratory Rate: ___________ /min
- Temperature: ___________ °C
- SpO$_2$ (on room air): ___________ %

Systemic Examination:

1. **Inspection:**

2. **Palpation:**

3. **Percussion:**

18. **Auscultation:**

19. **Other System Examination:**

Provisional Diagnosis:

Plan of Management:

Investigations :

Treatment :

Discussion

Case Record Template

Patient Name :   Age : Gender: IP No :

Occupation :   Address:

Chief Complaints:

1.

2.

3.

History of Present Illness:

History of Present Illness

Past History

☐ Hypertension (______ yrs)
☐ Diabetes Mellitus (______ yrs)
☐ Tuberculosis (______ yrs)
☐ Bronchial Asthma / COPD (______ yrs)
☐ ischemic heart disease (______ yrs)
☐ Stroke / TIA (______ yrs)
☐ Seizure Disorder (______ yrs)
☐ Chronic kidney disease (______ yrs)
☐ Others: ____________ ____________ ____________

☐ Thyroid Disorders (______ yrs)
☐ Hepatitis / Liver Disease (______ yrs)
☐ Malignancy (Specify): __________ (______ yrs)
☐ Previous Surgeries: ________ (Year: ______)
☐ Hospitalizations: __________ (Year: ______)
☐ Allergies (Drugs/Food): __________
☐ Blood Transfusions: ________ (Year: ______)

____________ ____________ ____________ __ ____________ ____________

____________ ____________ ____________ ____________ ____________

Personal History

☐ Marital Status: ☐ Single ☐ Married ☐ Widowed ☐ Divorced
Addictions:
☐ Smoking (______ yrs) (Type / Quantity): ________________________________
☐ Alcohol (______ yrs) (Type / Quantity): ____________________________ CAGE : ______
☐ Others (Specify): ____ (______ yrs)
☐ Dietary pattern: ☐ Vegetarian ☐ non-vegetarian
☐ Physical activity: ☐ Sedentary ☐ Moderate ☐ Active
☐ Others : __________ ____________________ ____________________
____ (______ yrs)

Menstrual & Obstetric History (if applicable)

☐ Age at menarche: __________ years
☐ Cycle length: __________ days
☐ Duration of bleeding: __________ days
☐ Regular cycles: ☐ Yes ☐ No
☐ Presence of clots: ☐ Yes ☐ No
☐ Obstetric history: G__ P__ L__ A__
☐ Last menstrual period (LMP): __________
☐ Menopause: ☐ Not attained ☐ Attained (age: ______ yrs)
Other : ________________________________

☐ Dysmenorrhea: ☐ Mild ☐ Moderate ☐ Severe
☐ Intermenstrual bleeding: ☐ Yes ☐ No
☐ Vaginal discharge: ☐ Yes (Describe): __________ ☐ No

____

Family History

☐ Hypertension (Relation: ____________)

☐ Diabetes Mellitus (Relation: __________)

☐ Coronary Artery Disease (Relation: ______)

☐ Stroke (Relation: __________)

☐ Others: ____

☐ Epilepsy (Relation: __________)

☐ Tuberculosis (Relation: __________)

☐ Cancer (Specify / Relation): __________

☐ Genetic / Inherited Disorders: __________

Drug History

☐ Regular medication use:

☐ Antihypertensives (_____ yrs)

☐ Antidiabetics (_____ yrs)

☐ Steroids (_____ yrs)

☐ Antiepileptics (_____ yrs)

☐ Anticoagulants / Antiplatelets (_____ yrs)

☐ Drug allergies (Specify): ____

☐ Immunosuppressants (_____ yrs)

☐ Others: __________ (_____ yrs)

☐ Over-the-counter medications (_____ yrs)

☐ Herbal / Alternative medicines (_____ yrs)

☐ Recent change in medications (Specify):

____

Summary :

Differential Diagnosis:

1. ___________________________

2. ___________________________

3. ___________________________

General Examination

☐ Conscious ☐ Drowsy ☐ Unconscious

☐ Coherent ☐ Incoherent

☐ Pallor: ☐ Present ☐ Absent

☐ Icterus: ☐ Present ☐ Absent

☐ Cyanosis: ☐ Present ☐ Absent

☐ Other findings: ____

☐ Clubbing: ☐ Present (Grade: ___) ☐ Absent

☐ Pedal Edema: ☐ Present ☐ Absent

☐ Generalized Lymphadenopathy: ☐ Present ☐ Absent

Vitals

- Pulse: ___________ /min, ____ Regular/Irregular, ____ Rhythm, ____ Volume, ____ Character, ☐ All peripheral pulses felt, ☐ No radio-radial delay, ☐ No radio-femoral delay, Other findings: ___________________
- Blood Pressure: ___________ mmHg
- Respiratory Rate: __________ /min
- Temperature: __________ °C
- SpO_2 (on room air): __________ %

Systemic Examination:

1. **Inspection:**

2. **Palpation:**

3. **Percussion:**

20. **Auscultation:**

21. **Other System Examination:**

Provisional Diagnosis:

Plan of Management:

Investigations :

Treatment :

Discussion

www.ingramcontent.com/pod-product-compliance
Lightning Source LLC
Chambersburg PA
CBHW041732100726
47973CB00011B/182